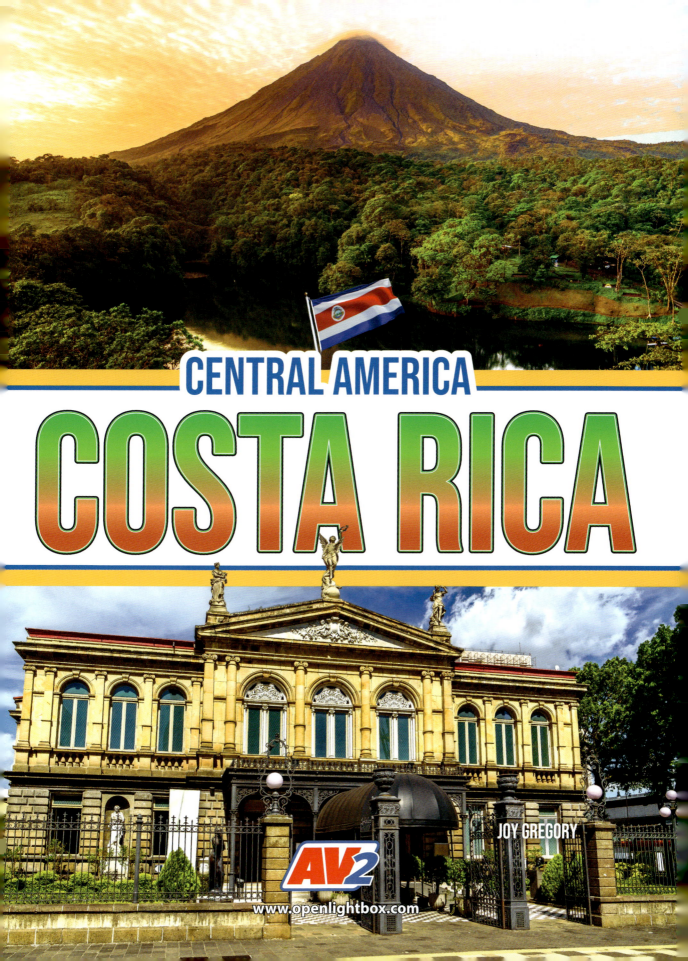

Step 1
Go to www.openlightbox.com

Step 2
Enter this unique code

AVC85699

Step 3
Explore your interactive eBook!

AV2 is optimized for use on any device

Your interactive eBook comes with...

Contents
Browse a live contents page to easily navigate through resources

Audio
Listen to sections of the book read aloud

Videos
Watch informative video clips

Weblinks
Gain additional information for research

Slideshows
View images and captions

Try This!
Complete activities and hands-on experiments

Key Words
Study vocabulary, and complete a matching word activity

Quizzes
Test your knowledge

Share
Share titles within your Learning Management System (LMS) or Library Circulation System

Citation
Create bibliographical references following APA, CMOS, and MLA styles

This title is part of our AV2 digital subscription

1-Year Grades K–5 Subscription
ISBN 978-1-7911-3320-7

Access hundreds of AV2 titles with our digital subscription.
Sign up for a FREE trial at **www.openlightbox.com/trial**

The digital components of this book are guaranteed to stay active for at least five years from the date of publication.

CENTRAL AMERICA
COSTA RICA

CONTENTS

Interactive eBook Code 2
Welcome to Costa Rica 4
Sites and Symbols 6
Exploring Costa Rica 8
Land and Climate 10
Plants and Animals 12
Economy 14
Tourism 16
Early Inhabitants 18
Settlement 19
From Colony to Country 20
Politics and Government 22
Population 23
Cultural Groups 24
Arts and Entertainment 26
Sports 28
Quiz Time 30
Key Words/Index 31

WELCOME TO COSTA RICA

Costa Rica is one of the countries that make up Central America. It is located on the **Isthmus** of Panama, a thin stretch of land connecting North and South America. Also known as the Republic of Costa Rica, the country is the oldest **democracy** in the region. It is also one of the most peaceful countries in Central America. Costa Rica is known for its scenery. More than 100 volcanoes dot the land, and several of them are still active. Costa Rica's mountains, forests, and beaches attract millions of tourists every year.

Eye on Costa Rica

Capital
San José

Population
5.2 million (2024 estimate)

Official Language
Spanish

National Coat of Arms

National Flag

National Anthem
"*Noble patria, tu hermosa bandera*" ("Noble Homeland, Your Beautiful Flag")

Currency
Costa Rican Colón (CRC)

SITES AND SYMBOLS

Costa Rica has its own unique identity. It uses a variety of symbols to represent this identity to the world. These symbols showcase the people, history, culture, and natural beauty of the country.

What's in a Name?
Historians say Costa Rica was named by European explorer Christopher Columbus. He landed in what is now Costa Rica in 1502. Costa rica is Spanish for "rich coast." Columbus gave the land this name because he thought it had an abundance of precious metals. Even though this was later proven to be untrue, the name remained.

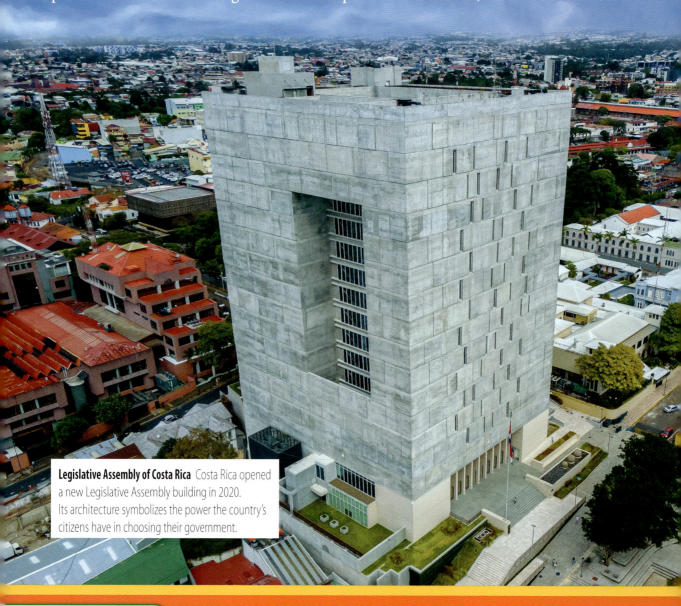

Legislative Assembly of Costa Rica Costa Rica opened a new Legislative Assembly building in 2020. Its architecture symbolizes the power the country's citizens have in choosing their government.

National Tree
The guanacaste tree was named Costa Rica's national tree in 1959. Also called the elephant ear tree, its shape is said to represent a government protecting its people.

National Bird
The yigüirro, or clay-colored thrush, has been Costa Rica's official bird since 1976. It is found throughout the country and stands as a symbol of Earth's **fertility**.

National Animal
In 2021, Costa Rica chose the sloth as its national animal. These sweet-natured, slow-moving animals represent the easygoing personality of the Costa Rican people.

National Flower
The Guaria Morada was designated as Costa Rica's national flower in 1939. It is said to symbolize the beauty of Costa Rican women.

EXPLORING COSTA RICA

Costa Rica covers 19,730 square miles (51,000 square kilometers) of land. The country is 288 miles (464 km) from north to south. It shares its northern border with Nicaragua and its southern border with Panama. Costa Rica has about 800 miles (1,287 km) of coastline. Its western boundary is shaped by the Pacific Ocean, while its eastern coast rests against the Caribbean Sea. At the country's narrowest point, these two bodies of water are only about 75 miles (121 km) apart.

① San José

Costa Rica's capital is also its most populated city. More than 335,000 people live in the city itself. The area around San José has about 1.1 million residents. San José was founded in about 1737. The city is located on major inland transportation routes. These roads travel north–south and east–west.

② Monteverde Cloud Forest Biological Reserve

The Monteverde **Cloud Forest** Biological Preserve is the largest cloud forest in Central America. Heavy mist and clouds almost always hang in the air. The preserve covers 35,089 acres (14,200 hectares) of forest. It protects 400 **species** of birds, 100 different **mammal** species, and 2,000 species of plants.

③ Mount Chirripó

Mount Chirripó is the tallest mountain in Costa Rica, reaching 12,530 feet (3,819 meters) above sea level. The mountain is found in southern Costa Rica, where it is part of the Talamanca Mountain Range. This range became a **UNESCO World Heritage Site** in 1983, ensuring its protection for future generations.

④ Arenal Volcano

Arenal Volcano is located in Arenal Volcano National Park, in northwestern Costa Rica. It measures 5,437 feet (1,657 m) above sea level. Until it entered a resting phase in 2010, this volcano was the most active in the country. Today, tourists visit the park to hike and to bathe in its hot springs.

LAND AND CLIMATE

Costa Rica was created by a row of underwater volcanoes that began erupting more than 3 million years ago. The eruptions spewed molten rock that rose to the water's surface. Over time, this rock accumulated to form the Isthmus of Panama, the land on which Costa Rica now sits.

Volcanic activity also contributed to the formation of Costa Rica's four main mountain ranges. All of these ranges run down the middle of the country. The Guanacaste Mountains are located in the north. The Tilarán and Central Mountain ranges are closer to the country's middle, where they help to shape Costa Rica's Central Valley. The Talamanca Mountains are farther south. They have the country's steepest terrain.

The mountains give way to lowlands on either side. However, each side of the country has its own features. The Caribbean coastal area has **mangroves** and swamps. The Pacific coastline is rockier with high cliffs in some areas.

Many of Costa Rica's volcanoes have craters, or bowl-shaped formations, in their peaks. Often, a crater fills with water when the volcano is not erupting.

The San Juan River is the longest river in Costa Rica. It flows south 124 miles (200 km) from the border with Nicaragua to the Caribbean Sea.

Braulio Carrillo National Park, on the east coast of Costa Rica, gets up to 16.5 feet (5 m) of rain a year.

Costa Rica has two main climate zones. Both are influenced by the country's location near the **equator**. Northern areas along the Pacific coast have a tropical climate. This means they are hot year-round and have two seasons. The dry season runs from December to April, while the wet season is typically from May to November. This is when most of the area's rain falls. The eastern side of Costa Rica and the southern part along the Pacific coast have an equatorial climate. The temperatures here are warm, with rainfall evenly distributed throughout the year.

Seasonal Costa Rica

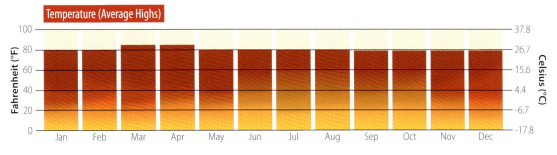

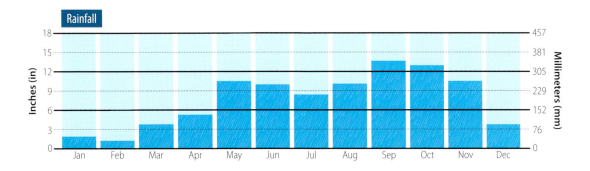

PLANTS AND ANIMALS

Costa Rica has about 500,000 different plant and animal species. This is more than 5 percent of all the plant and animal species in the world. More than 2,000 kinds of trees can be found in Costa Rica. The kapok tree is sometimes referred to as the "giant of the **rainforest**." This is because it can grow to be more than 200 feet (61 m) tall.

More than 9,000 species of flowering plants can be found in Costa Rica, including at least 1,200 kinds of orchids. Heliconias and birds-of-paradise are also common. Several types of flowering epiphytes grow in Costa Rica's rainforests. Sometimes called air plants, epiphytes grow on top of other plants. They receive their moisture and nutrients from the air and water around them rather than by growing roots in the soil.

More than 800 kinds of ferns grow in Costa Rica's rainforests.

The kapok tree is a deciduous tree. It sheds its leaves when Costa Rica's dry season moves in.

12 CENTRAL AMERICA

🇨🇷 Margays are primarily tree dwellers. Their flexible toes and ankles allow them to move stealthily through the trees when hunting.

Costa Rica has in excess of 230 mammal species. The country's most common mammals are bats, monkeys, and coatis. Six kinds of wild cats, including the jaguar and margay, also make their home there. Snakes are Costa Rica's most common type of reptile. Some, such as the bushmaster, are venomous. This snake is the largest venomous snake in the Western Hemisphere. It can measure up to 12 feet (3.7 m) long. The country also has more than 900 species of birds. Many, including the scarlet macaw and the resplendent quetzal, are very colorful.

🇨🇷 Scarlet macaws mate for life and are often spotted in pairs.

Costa Rica Bits

Costa Rica has at least **200 species** of reptiles.

Almost **10 percent** of Costa Rica's plants are found only in that country.

The Dutchman's pipe is the **largest flower** in Costa Rica. Its blooms can grow up to **8 inches** (20 centimeters) long.

COSTA RICA 13

ECONOMY

Most businesses in Costa Rica are privately owned. However, the Costa Rican government does own and operate utility companies. These are companies that supply electricity and water. The government also owns the country's shipping ports and railroads.

The service sector is a major contributor to Costa Rica's **gross domestic product (GDP)**. This sector provides services instead of goods. Many of the country's service jobs are in banking and tourism. Service workers also work in transportation and construction.

Costa Rica has an active agriculture industry. Its main agricultural **exports** are bananas and pineapples. The country also exports coffee and sugar. Other agricultural exports include macadamia nuts and cut flowers. An increasing number of farms are growing **organic foods**.

In mountainous areas, farmers cut terraces, or steps, into the hillsides to create flat land for crops.

Costa Rica has about 50,000 small coffee farms. In 2023, the country's coffee exports hit $456 million USD.

Located along Costa Rica's eastern coast, the Port of Limón is the country's largest seaport. Approximately 1.1 million tons (1 million metric tons) of cargo pass through it every year.

Most of Costa Rica's fishing industry is concentrated in the waters off the Pacific coast. Tuna and shrimp are the main catches. The country now also relies on **aquaculture** for its fish supplies. Costa Rica's fish farms grow most of the tilapia sold to export markets.

Industries that make goods account for about 20 percent of Costa Rica's economy. Medical equipment, construction materials, and plastic products are among the country's many manufactured goods. Some companies make parts for aerospace, automotive, and electronic industries. Most factories are located in and around San José, with smaller centers in the cities of Puntarenas and Limón. Most of Costa Rica's manufactured goods are exported to other countries.

In 2023, the country exported approximately $18.2 billion worth of goods. The United States is Costa Rica's largest trading partner. It receives about 40 percent of Costa Rica's exports. In return, approximately 39 percent of the products Costa Rica **imports** come from the United States. These include oil and gas.

Costa Rica GDP by Sector

Costa Rica has a GDP of about $100 billion. Services, industry, and agriculture are the biggest contributors.

Services 68%
Industry 21%
Other 7%
Agriculture 4%

TOURISM

Costa Rica is one of the most popular tourist destinations in Central America. The country welcomes more than 2 million people a year. Tourist spending generates close to $5 billion USD annually for the country. Most visitors to Costa Rica are from the United States and Canada. Tourist numbers spike from December to April, when temperatures in those countries are colder.

Almost 80 percent of the tourists who visit Costa Rica participate in **ecotourism** activities. This allows them to learn about the country's natural environment and the efforts being made to conserve it for future generations. Many of these activities focus on the **biodiversity** found within Costa Rica.

Visitors interested in ecotourism often spend time in Costa Rica's national parks and protected areas. Wildlife reserves also attract many international travelers. Ballena National Marine Park, along Costa Rica's west coast, is the place to see humpback whales and dolphins frolicking in the water. Birdwatchers head to Palo Verde National Park hoping to see some of the more than 300 bird species that live there.

Most international visitors to Costa Rica transit through Juan Santamaria International Airport, just outside San José.

The Hanging Bridges of Arenal, near Arenal National Park, provide a bird's-eye view of the rainforest. The 2-mile (3-km) trail includes 16 bridges in total.

Costa Rica Bits

Costa Rica is home to **34 national parks** and **protected areas**.

In 2024, **6** out of every **10 tourists** visiting Costa Rica came from the **United States**.

Close to **360,000 people** visit Manuel Antonio National Park every year. It is the **most popular** park in Costa Rica.

Adventurous tourists enjoy water activities such as surfing and whitewater rafting. Others plan trips around one of Costa Rica's many festivals, which often feature music, dancing, and rodeos. Rainforest and volcano tours are other major attractions. At La Paz Waterfall Gardens, tourists can hike to five waterfalls. Along the way, they will see tropical flowers, trees, and other plants. Tourists interested in Costa Rican history can visit its museums and old churches. Some of the most popular museums are in San José.

Costa Rica has three UNESCO World Heritage Sites preserving natural wonders. The Guanacaste Conservation Area includes nesting areas for sea turtles. La Amistad National Park has Central America's tallest non-volcanic mountain peaks. Cocos Island, off the Pacific coast, supports a variety of plants and animals, several of which are **endemic**.

Costa Rica celebrates Independence Day on September 15. Parades featuring local children are a big part of the celebration.

Cocos Island is located 340 miles (547 km) off the Pacific coast of Costa Rica. The World Heritage Site's 20 dive sites give visitors the opportunity to swim close to at least 30 species of coral and 300 species of fish.

EARLY INHABITANTS

People have lived in Central America for more than 12,000 years. The earliest inhabitants were hunter-gatherers. Their **ancestors** came to North America from Asia, slowly following the animals they hunted south. Over time, some of these people reached Central America and settled there.

By 5000 BC, these groups were beginning to abandon their **nomadic** lifestyle in favor of becoming agricultural societies. Some began growing their own food. Others kept wild pigs. Most people lived in small huts made from nearby plants. **Archaeologists** have found some of the clay pots and utensils these groups used for cooking. They have identified tools made from bones and stone.

Other ancient objects found indicate that some of these early peoples were craftspeople as well. Some made beads from shells. They then used these beads to create jewelry. Others sculpted objects from wood or clay. A market for these items began to develop. People traded among themselves and with other groups. A trading network formed as a result.

Costa Rica's round stone monuments are a mystery. Found on the Diquis Delta and Isla del Cano, scientists believe they marked special places.

The Guayabo National Monument, in the Central Valley, preserves the remains of a pre-Columbian settlement that is believed to have been built about 3,000 years ago.

SETTLEMENT

By 500 AD, Costa Rica was divided into several kingdoms, each made up of several villages. Every kingdom had one chief, or ruler. This person set the laws for the people living there. Villagers organized markets, where they traded food and goods. Religion had become an important part of daily life at this time, and each kingdom had its own religious leaders and healers.

As the kingdoms evolved, trade routes took shape. These gave people a way to exchange food and goods across greater distances. Most routes were organized along coasts and rivers. This is where most of the villages were located. Traders moved goods from settlement to settlement. Jade is one of the goods that came into Costa Rica from other parts of Central America. People used it to make jewelry and art. As jade is very strong, it was also used to make tools and weapons.

Scientists believe that, by the time Christopher Columbus arrived in the New World in 1492, Costa Rica was under the control of four main **Indigenous** groups. These were the Borucas, Caribs, Chibchas, and Diquis. Each of these groups had its own customs and way of life.

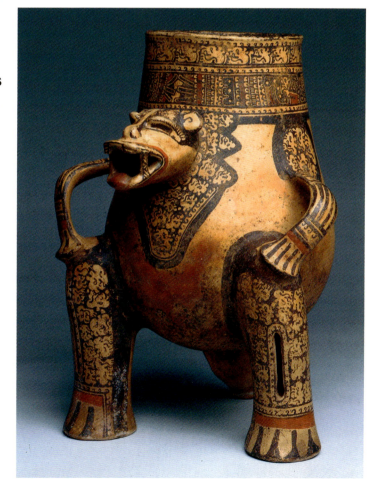

About 1,000 years ago, people in the Nicoya Peninsula region were creating ceramic cups decorated with figures of animals such as jaguars.

FROM COLONY TO COUNTRY

The Spanish Empire took control of Costa Rica in about 1560. **New Spain** included countries in modern-day Central America, along with Mexico and parts of the United States. Over time, people from Africa, South Asia, and China were brought to Costa Rica, arriving as slaves and servants. By the early 1800s, Spain had established several **colonies** in Costa Rica.

In 1821, Spain lost control of Central America. Two years later, Costa Rica became part of the United Provinces of Central America. El Salvador, Guatemala, Honduras, and Nicaragua were also members. Costa Rica became an independent country in 1838.

In the early 1900s, Costa Rica experienced political unrest. A brief **civil war** took place in 1948, following a national election that many felt was fraudulent. By 1949, Costa Rica had a new, democratic **constitution**. Since the military had fought in the civil war, it was abolished. In its place, Costa Rica set up a national police force.

Bellavista Fortress was built in 1917 as barracks, or housing for military personnel. Today, it is the Costa Rica National Museum.

COSTA RICA TIMELINE

10,000 BC–500 AD

FIRST PEOPLES
Ancient peoples settle in what is now Costa Rica.

About 1560

SPAIN IN CHARGE
Spain takes control of Costa Rica. The region becomes part of New Spain.

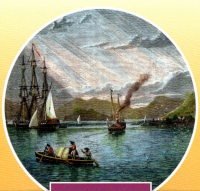

1821–1838

AN INDEPENDENT NATION
After Central America gains independence from Spain, Costa Rica works to become an independent country.

20 CENTRAL AMERICA

The 1949 constitution introduced many programs that made life better for Costa Rican citizens. Its new laws protected children and seniors. It also introduced minimum wages and workers' rights. The constitution gave women and people of African ancestry the right to vote. It put banks under the government's control.

Lawyer and businessman José Figueres Ferrer led the uprising against the Costa Rican government in 1948. He was elected president in 1953 and 1970.

By the 1980s, different political groups were fighting for power in Central America. This kept investors and tourists out of Costa Rica. In 1987, Costa Rica's president, Óscar Arias Sánchez, negotiated a peace plan among the warring factions. It was signed by Nicaragua, El Salvador, Guatemala, and Honduras. President Sanchez won a **Nobel Peace Prize** for his work.

Life in Costa Rica improved as a result of this agreement. Poverty decreased, and the government spent more money on education. More people learned to read and write. By the 1990s, tourism was booming, and foreign investors were opening firms in Costa Rica.

1949 — A NEW CONSTITUTION
Costa Rica passes a new constitution, which establishes elections and voting rights.

1987 — NOBEL PRIZE WINNER
President Óscar Arias Sánchez wins the Nobel Peace Prize for his work in Central America.

2024 — HISTORY RETURNED
Almost 400 **artifacts** taken from Costa Rica are returned by museums in the United States. These include pottery, art., and jade jewelry.

POLITICS AND GOVERNMENT

Costa Rica elects its government every four years. All citizens over 18 are required to vote. Voters elect the president, two vice-presidents, and a Legislative Assembly. The president can only serve one four-year term. Eight years after that term has ended, he or she is allowed to run again. Most members of the legislature are members of a political party.

As the head of government, the president leads the Legislative Assembly. The assembly has 57 elected members. Their job is to write and approve laws. The president appoints some of these members to oversee particular areas of government business, such as agriculture and education. These people are called cabinet ministers. Costa Rica's president also acts as the country's head of state. This role requires the president to represent the country abroad.

Costa Rica has an independent judicial system. Its Supreme Court has 22 judges. They are elected by the Legislative Assembly. Each judge serves an eight-year term. When that term ends, judges can run again.

Rodrigo Chaves was elected Costa Rica's president in 2022. He is the 49th person to hold the position.

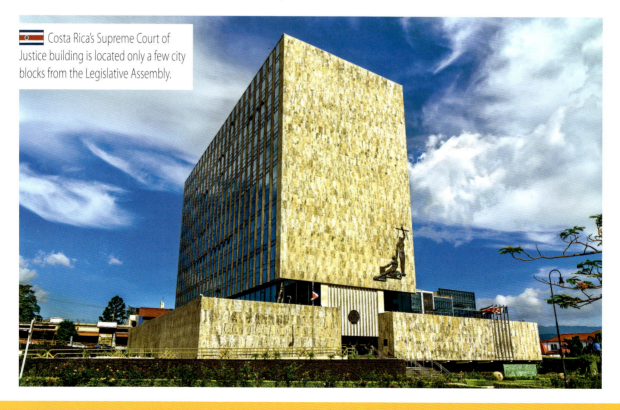

Costa Rica's Supreme Court of Justice building is located only a few city blocks from the Legislative Assembly.

POPULATION

By 2024, Costa Rica had a population of more than 5 million people. About 83 percent of them live in **urban** areas. However, San José is the only city with more than 300,000 people. Today, about 9 percent of Costa Rica's population was born outside of the country. Most of these people moved to Costa Rica from other parts of Central America.

About 20 percent of Costa Rica's population lives in poverty. In most countries, this would lower **life expectancy**. This is not the case here. In 1950, the life expectancy in Costa Rica was 54.4 years. However, by the late 1970s, the government had improved access to health care, clean water, and electricity. By 2024, the country's average life expectancy was 81. This is higher than that of some countries with less poverty.

Education for Kindergarten to Grade 12 students has also improved in recent years. Costa Rica has a **literacy rate** of 96 percent. Still, school dropout rates are high. About 22 percent of students do not finish Grade 12. This is higher in **rural** areas. These regions have fewer schools, and more people live in poverty.

Located on the Caribbean Sea, the city of Limón is Costa Rica's second-largest city, after San José. Limón has a population of about 63,000.

Poverty rates are highest among Costa Rica's Indigenous people. Their children are less likely to attend Kindergarten or finish Grade 12.

CULTURAL GROUPS

Most Costa Ricans have European ancestry, mainly Spanish. However, almost 20 percent of the population has mixed heritage, with both Indigenous and European ancestors. About 2 percent of Costa Ricans belong to one of the country's eight different Indigenous groups. Another 1 percent of the population has Black ancestors.

Spanish is the official language of Costa Rica. Most children now study English at school. Several Indigenous groups still speak their own languages. Some Costa Ricans with African ancestors speak Spanish and Limonese Creole. This language was developed among African slaves.

Costa Rica's constitution guarantees freedom of religion. **Roman Catholicism** is the country's official religion. The Spanish introduced it to Central America in the early days of their arrival. Today, about 75 percent of Costa Ricans are Roman Catholic. Most of the remainder are Protestants. Some Indigenous groups practice their own religions.

Located in Cártago, Our Lady of the Angels Basilica honors Mary, the patron saint of Costa Rica. The church, which was built for the city's Roman Catholic worshipers, was completed in 1930.

Costa Rica hosts dozens of festivals each year. Many are tied to the Catholic church calendar. Most of these religious festivals are held near Easter and Christmas. Businesses often close to allow people to celebrate holy days with parades and music. Other festivals are related to local customs and traditions. Rodeos, for instance, play an important role in the festivals of the Guanacaste region. This is because the area is known for its cattle ranches.

Bullfighting, also called bull taming in Costa Rica, is a popular rodeo sport. Bulls and riders show their strength and agility.

Rice and beans are staples of the Costa Rican diet. Most people eat gallo pinto for breakfast. This rice and bean dish is flavored with peppers, onions, and garlic, and is sometimes served with fried eggs. Casado is a popular lunch dish. It is made with white rice, black or red beans, vegetables, and chicken or beef. Most Costa Rican food is not very spicy. In some parts of the country, dishes are flavored with coconut. In other areas, cilantro is more common.

Casado is a common menu item in restaurants across Costa Rica.

Costa Rica Bits

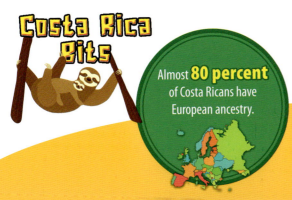

Almost **80 percent** of Costa Ricans have European ancestry.

The **Palmares Festival** is Costa Rica's **longest festival**. It lasts for **2 weeks** every January.

¡Hola!
Approximately **11 percent** of all Costa Ricans speak a **second language**.

ARTS AND ENTERTAINMENT

Costa Rica has an active theater scene. Some of the best-known theaters are in San José. The National Theater is known for both its stunning architecture and the many concerts it holds throughout the year. The Melico Salazar Theater is one of the country's largest theaters. It was built in 1928 to stage **operettas** but now hosts a wide range of artistic performances.

Several museums and galleries celebrate the visual arts. The Museum of Contemporary Art and Design, in San José, focuses on art made by artists from Central America. The Costa Rican Art Museum, also in San José, displays pieces by well-known artists from Costa Rica. It has an outdoor sculpture garden as well.

The National Theater's interior is just as opulent as the exterior, with bronze lamp fixtures and walls decorated in gold leaf.

Francisco Zúñiga, originally from San José, is a world-renowned sculptor. In addition to Costa Rica, his work has been exhibited in Mexico, New York, and Washington, DC.

Some of the country's museums show art produced before the Spanish arrived. The National Museum of Costa Rica is one of the largest. It has **artifacts** dating back 2,400 years. The Museum of Jade also highlights pre-Columbian times. Its collection includes more than 7,000 pieces of art made from jade, ceramic, and stone.

The Museum of Jade, in San José, holds the world's largest collection of American jade.

Costa Rican traditional music was influenced by Spanish and African rhythms and sounds. The country chose the marimba as its national musical instrument in 1996. This percussion instrument was likely introduced by African slaves in the 18th century. Many traditional songs feature a wind instrument called the ocarina. Most ocarinas are shaped like animals. The chirimía is another wind instrument heard in Costa Rican music. It is similar to the oboe. Oboes were brought to Costa Rica by Spanish priests. Both chirimías and oboes have been played at religious events for centuries.

Debi Nova is one of Costa Rica's most celebrated singers and songwriters. She has won numerous accolades for her music, including six Grammy nominations.

SPORTS

Soccer is the most popular sport in Costa Rica. It was introduced by English settlers. The country has a professional men's league with 12 teams. The national men's team is the most successful soccer team in Central America and has won numerous tournaments. The team finished fourth at the 2014 FIFA World Cup, the sport's most important international competition. In 2021, Costa Rica finished fourth at the CONCACAF Nations League. That league includes teams from North America.

Goalkeeper Keylor Navas was in net when Costa Rica's national team reached the quarterfinals at the 2014 World Cup.

Costa Rica has also earned sports honors in other events. The country has won four Olympic medals since 1988. This includes a gold medal won by Claudia Poll Ahrens for swimming in 1996. Nery Brenes is one of the country's best sprinters, winning gold in the 400-meter at the 2012 Indoor World Championships in Istanbul, Türkiye. Andrey Amador is recognized as one of Costa Rica's best cyclists. Before retiring, he competed in major bike races around the world.

Nery Brenes won the 2012 IAAF Indoor World Championship 400-meter final with a time of 45.11 seconds.

Basketball has been gaining popularity in Costa Rica in recent years. The country has both a men's and women's national team. They play mostly against teams from the Caribbean and other Central American countries. The Costa Rican National Basketball League formed in 2005. It helps promote the game's popularity with young people. Like soccer, basketball only requires a ball and shoes. This makes it an accessible sport for many young players.

La Ruta de Los Conquistadores is Costa Rica's premier mountain bike race, and one of the most difficult races in the world. Covering a distance of 161 miles (259 km), this 3-day race snakes through tropical rainforests, banana plantations, and tiny farm towns.

Fighting sports are popular in Costa Rica. Some of the country's best-known boxers are women. Hanna Gabriels Valle and Yokasta Galeth Valle Álvarez have both been named world champions in multiple weight categories. Many of the country's local gyms teach boxing. Others teach martial arts such as taekwondo and jiu jitsu.

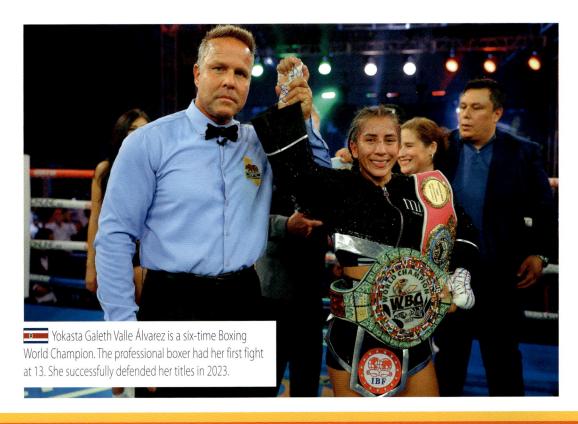
Yokasta Galeth Valle Álvarez is a six-time Boxing World Champion. The professional boxer had her first fight at 13. She successfully defended her titles in 2023.

QUIZ TIME

Test your knowledge of Costa Rica by answering these questions.

1 How many volcanoes does Costa Rica have?

2 What does *costa rica* mean in English?

3 What is the name of Costa Rica's capital city?

4 What is the national religion of Costa Rica?

5 Which two foods are staples of the Costa Rican diet?

6 In which year did Costa Rica become an independent country?

7 Which Costa Rican president won a Nobel Peace Prize?

8 What is Costa Rica's most popular sport?

9 What is the highest mountain in Costa Rica?

10 What is Costa Rica's official language?

ANSWERS
1. More than 100
2. "Rich coast"
3. San José
4. Roman Catholicism
5. Rice and beans
6. 1838
7. Oscar Arias Sánchez
8. Soccer
9. Mount Chirripó
10. Spanish

30 CENTRAL AMERICA

KEY WORDS

ancestors: members of one's cultural group or family who lived in the past
aquaculture: the farming of fish and other seafood
archaeologists: scientists who study human history, often by examining ancient objects
artifacts: objects made by humans in the past
biodiversity: the variety of life in a particular place
civil war: a war between citizens of the same country
cloud forest: a humid tropical forest that has almost constant cloud cover
colonies: settlements controlled by another country
constitution: a document establishing a country's form of government and the powers of the government
democracy: a government elected by free and fair elections
ecotourism: tourism activities that do not harm the natural environment
endemic: native and restricted to a certain place
equator: an imaginary line around the center of Earth
exports: goods sold to another country
fertility: the ability to support the growth of a large number of strong, healthy plants
gross domestic product (GDP): the total value of all the goods and services produced in a country's economy
imports: brings in goods from other countries
Indigenous: the original people of a particular place
isthmus: a narrow strip of land connecting two larger land areas
life expectancy: the number of years, on average, that people in a population group can expect to live
literacy rate: the number of people over 15 years of age who can read and write well enough to manage everyday work and life
mammal: an animal that has hair or fur and drinks its mother's milk
mangroves: forests with trees that grow in salty water
New Spain: the former Spanish possessions in the Western Hemisphere
Nobel Peace Prize: an international award in honor of people who work for peace
nomadic: roaming from place to place
operettas: short operas that are typically light and comical in character
organic foods: edible products that are free of artificial food additives
rainforest: a wooded area with broadleaf evergreen trees that receives at least 100 inches (254 cm) of rain a year
Roman Catholicism: relating to the Christian church of which the Pope, or bishop of Rome, is the supreme head
rural: relating to the countryside
species: a set of animals or plants in which the members have similar characteristics
UNESCO World Heritage Site: a place that has been determined to be of global importance by the United Nations Educational, Scientific, and Cultural Organization, whose main goals are to promote world peace and eliminate poverty through education, science, and culture
urban: relating to cities and towns

INDEX

Ahrens, Claudia Maria Poll 28
Álvarez, Yokasta Galeth Valle 29
Amador, Andrey 28
animals 7, 9, 12, 13, 15, 16, 17, 18, 19, 25, 27

Bellavista Fortress 20
Brenes, Nery 28

Caribbean Sea 8, 10, 23
climate 10, 11, 16
Columbus, Christopher 6, 19
constitution 20, 21, 24

economy 14, 15

Ferrer, José Figueres 21

government 6, 7, 14, 21, 22, 23

language 5, 24, 25

Olympics 28

mountains 4, 9, 10, 14, 17, 30
museums 17, 20, 21, 22, 26, 27

Pacific Ocean 8, 10, 15, 17
plants 7, 9, 12, 13, 14, 16, 17, 18

rainforest 12, 16, 17, 29
religion 17, 19, 24, 25, 30

Sánchez, Óscar Arias 21, 30
San José 5, 9, 15, 16, 17, 23, 26, 27, 30
sports 28, 29

tourism 4, 9, 14, 16, 17, 21

Valle, Hanna Gabriels 29
volcanoes 4, 9, 10, 17, 30

waterfalls 17

Get the best of both worlds.

AV2 bridges the gap between print and digital.

The expandable resources toolbar enables quick access to content including **videos**, **audio**, **activities**, **weblinks**, **slideshows**, **quizzes**, and **key words**.

Animated videos make static images come alive.

Resource icons on each page help readers to further **explore key concepts**.

Published by Lightbox Learning Inc.
276 5th Avenue, Suite 704 #917
New York, NY 10001
Website: www.openlightbox.com

Copyright ©2026 Lightbox Learning Inc.
All rights reserved. No part of this publication may be reproduced, stored in a retrieval system, or transmitted in any form or by any means, electronic, mechanical, photocopying, recording, or otherwise, without the prior written permission of the publisher.

Library of Congress Cataloging-in-Publication Data
Names: Gregory, Joy author
Title: Costa Rica / Joy Gregory.
Description: New York, NY : Lightbox Learning Inc, [2026] | Series: Central America | Includes index. | Audience: Grades 4-6
Identifiers: LCCN 2025003987 (print) | LCCN 2025003988 (ebook) | ISBN 9798874519148 lib. bdg. | ISBN 9798874519155 paperback | ISBN 9798874519162 ebook other | ISBN 9798874519179 ebook other
Subjects: LCSH: Costa Rica--Juvenile literature
Classification: LCC F1543.2 .G74 2026 (print) | LCC F1543.2 (ebook) | DDC 972.86--dc23/eng/20250320
LC record available at https://lccn.loc.gov/2025003987
LC ebook record available at https://lccn.loc.gov/2025003988

Printed in Fargo, North Dakota, in the United States of America
1 2 3 4 5 6 7 8 9 0 29 28 27 26 25

052025
250516

Project Coordinator Heather Kissock
Designer Terry Paulhus
Layout Mandy Christiansen

The publisher has made every reasonable effort to trace ownership and to obtain permission to use copyright material. The publisher would be pleased to have any errors or omissions brought to its attention so that they may be corrected in subsequent printings. Some visual elements in this title may have been generated using AI. While we strive for accuracy in all aspects of our products, we cannot guarantee that the elements depicted in these images are accurate. The publisher acknowledges Getty Images, Alamy, Shutterstock, and Wikimedia Common as the primary image suppliers for this title. If you have any inquiries about these images or would like to provide any feedback, please reach out to us at feedback@openlightbox.com

All of the Internet URLs and Google Maps links given in the interactive eBook were valid at the time of publication. However, due to the dynamic nature of the Internet, some addresses may have changed, or sites may have ceased to exist since publication. While the author and publisher regret any inconvenience this may cause readers, no responsibility for any such changes can be accepted by either the author or the publisher.